You've Survived Catholic School When...

Written by Francis X. Andrews
Designed and Illustrated by Martin Riskin

Published simultaneously in Canada by
Marka Canada, Toronto, Ontario

Manufactured in the United States of America

30 29 28 27 26 25 24 23 22 21 20 19 18 17 16 15 14 13 12 11 10 9 8 7

IVORY TOWER PUBLISHING COMPANY, INC.
125 Walnut Street, Watertown, MA 02172
TEL: (617) 923-1111   TELEX: 262992 ITAP

You've Survived Catholic School When...

You come up to bat at the company softball game without crossing yourself.

You've Survived Catholic School When...

You don't shudder when someone
hands you a ruler.

You've Survived Catholic School When...

You pick up a girl at a singles bar
who is not wearing a crucifix.

You've Survived Catholic School When...

You finally feel comfortable wearing a pleated plaid jumper without white ankle socks.

You've Survived Catholic School When...

You stop believing God will strike you dead
if you go to a church of another religion.

You've Survived Catholic School When...

You no longer rush to confession
at the airport chapel.

You've Survived Catholic School When...

You find your lost Rosary beads and you can still do five decades in ten minutes.

You've Survived Catholic School When...

You're simply relieved that your daughter's
finally getting married, and you don't think
it's a sin he's not a Catholic.

You've Survived Catholic School When...

You put a pink flamingo on your lawn
next to the statue of the Blessed Mother.

You've Survived Catholic School When...

You take your family
to a steak house on Friday.

You've Survived
Catholic School When...

You know ejaculation is something else
besides a short, intense prayer.

You've Survived Catholic School When...

You buckle up even though
you still have a statue of St. Christopher.

You've Survived Catholic School When...

You can't give up anything for Lent
because you're already on a strict diet.

You've Survived Catholic School When...

You don't leave room for the Holy Ghost
during slow dances.

You've Survived Catholic School When...

You only go to Mass on Christmas and Easter.

You've Survived Catholic School When...

You still can't answer the questions
in the Baltimore Catechism.

You've Survived Catholic School When...

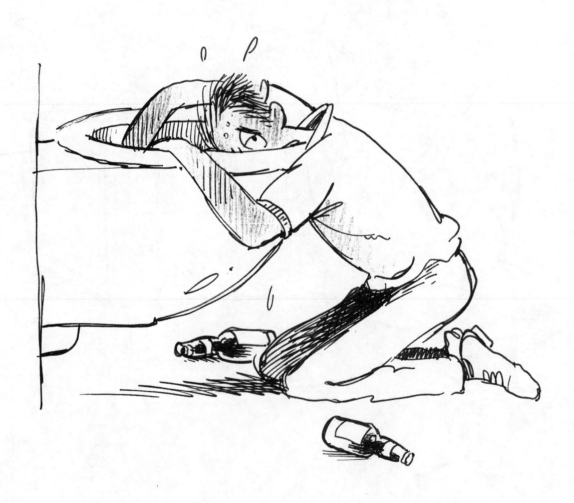

You forget that your body is
the Temple of the Holy Ghost.

You've Survived Catholic School When...

You remember fondly that August 15th
is a Holy Day of Obligation.

You've Survived Catholic School When...

You can't remember your last confession.

You've Survived Catholic School When...

Your daughter receives Communion
in sneakers.

You've Survived Catholic School When...

You say the Rosary while doing aerobics.

You've Survived Catholic School When...

You stay in bed after a heavy date
instead of running out to confession.

You've Survived
Catholic School When...

You fulfill your Easter Duty in the Caribbean.

You've Survived
Catholic School When...

Looking at the "National Geographic"
is no longer a near occasion of sin.

You've Survived Catholic School When...

You enter a phone booth without feeling
you should begin to confess.

You've Survived Catholic School When...

You meet your 5th grade nun
on a peace march.

You've Survived Catholic School When...

The rhythm method is something
your dancersize instructor tells you about.

You've Survived Catholic School When...

You see a priest buy a lottery ticket
instead of trying to sell one.

You've Survived Catholic School When...

You go to a movie without checking out
its Legion of Deceny rating.

You've Survived Catholic School When...

Limbo is a dance in the Caribbean
and not the destination of unbaptized children.

You've Survived Catholic School When...

You eat deli on Ash Wednesday.

You've Survived Catholic School When...

Your parish sponsors a trip to Las Vegas
instead of running Bingo nights.

You've Survived Catholic School When...

You no longer line up in places by size.

You've Survived Catholic School When...

You bet against Notre Dame
if the odds are right.

You've Survived Catholic School When...

Your idea of an indulgence changes.

You've Survived Catholic School When...

You only remember about 10 words of Latin.

You've Survived Catholic School When...

The hemlines on your short skirts
are not held up with Scotch tape.

You've Survived Catholic School When...

You eat breakfast before Mass.

You've Survived Catholic School When...

You realize there is no patron saint
for your profession.

You've Survived Catholic School When...

You often begin Sunday with a Bloody Mary instead of a Hail Mary.

You've Survived Catholic School When...

You stop worrying about wearing
patent leather shoes.

You've Survived Catholic School When...

You go to church without a hat.

You've Survived Catholic School When...

You realize your offering is tax deductible.

You've Survived Catholic School When...

St. Croix is your patron saint in the winter.

You've Survived Catholic School When...

Original sin sounds like fun.

You've Survived Catholic School When...

You decide to send your own kids
to Catholic School.